Jumpstarting

Nigeria's

Journey of

Greatness

Jumpstarting Nigeria's *Journey of* Greatness

Oluwaseun Sodipe

ISBN: 978-81-19524-24-2

First published in India in 2024 by Exceller Books,
An imprint of GE Group

Address: G1, Dream Apartment, Degree College Road, Belgharia, Kolkata, 700056, India

www.excellerbooks.com

Dedication

To Oluwatiseteminire Olivia Sodipe, and Ireoluwade Ivan Sodipe. I am grateful to God for giving you to us. I look forward, with hope and expectation, to what God has in store for the world through you.

To the Holy Spirit, for Your love, guidance, correction, support, and every other help rendered to me through the years, this is most especially for You.

Acknowledgement

To my Wife Oyinade

To my dearest wife, Oyinade, your patience and unwavering support have been the bedrock upon which this journey was built. Thank you, babe, for your understanding during moments of dedication, for being my source of encouragement when challenges arose, and for your boundless love that fueled my determination.

To my Teachers

To the educators who've nurtured my growth, your impact extends far beyond the classroom walls, from Mrs Aroloye, Mrs Nnanna, and Mrs Alarape, who were there when I was in nursery/primary school to professors. Oyelaran, Falode and Alabi, your guidance and wisdom have been instrumental in shaping my perspective. Your dedication to sharing knowledge has ignited the flame of curiosity within me, and for that, I'm deeply grateful.

To Fatima HZ, Seun "Bobo", Uncle Ayo, Uncle Biodun, Deji Ademefun, Jide Alawode, Priscilla, Femi Akande, Anderson Momoh, Belove Momoh, Grace Momoh, Elder & Deaconess Momoh, Aunty Esther Ikomi, Faosy, Wilson "Dr. Innocent", Mrs. Olaleye, Andrew "Sarkin Yaki", Omotoyosi "Madam Toyo", Kazeem "Boss", and Dr. Chukwugozie Ujam.

Your names are etched onto the pages of this book as symbols of friendship, encouragement, and collaboration. Your presence has been a testament to the power of connections and shared aspirations. Through discussions, insights, and shared experiences, you've contributed immeasurably to the depth and breadth of this work.

To Kayode, Opeoluwa, Alex, Ibijoke, and Modupe
Finally, to my parents – Kayode, Opeoluwa, Alex, Ibijoke, and Modupe – this journey is a testament to the values and principles you've instilled within me. Your unwavering support, encouragement, and belief in my potential have been the driving force behind this endeavour. Your love and guidance have not only shaped this book but have shaped the person I've become.

As I extend my gratitude to each name on this page, I'm reminded that our lives are a reflection of the connections we forge, the bonds we nurture, and the impact we leave behind. This acknowledgement is more than words; it's a heartfelt expression of appreciation for the collective effort that has brought this book to life. With deep thanks and a heart brimming with gratitude, I dedicate these words to each individual whose name graces this page. May our paths continue to intertwine, our bonds continue to strengthen, and our impact continues to resonate in the lives we touch.

Table of Contents

Growing Up in Nigeria
(The 90s and 2000)

I was born on March 13th 1986, in Lagos Island, Lagos State, Nigeria. For the first 5-6 years of my life, I was oblivious to all except God, family, school and play. Growing up in Nigeria in the 90s and 2000s was a unique experience that shaped the lives of many individuals, mine inclusive. It was a time of rapid change and transition for the country, with advancements in technology, the rise of globalisation, and the challenges of political instability. This chapter examines the various aspects of growing up in Nigeria during this period, including the cultural influences, educational system, and the impact of economic changes.

Cultural Influences

Nigeria is rich in cultural diversity, with over 250 ethnic groups. Growing up in Nigeria during the '90s and 2000s meant exposure to many cultural influences, especially through the electronic media. Traditional festivals and celebrations were an integral part of our upbringing, showcasing the vibrant music, dance, and art forms of different ethnic groups.

Nollywood, the Nigerian film industry, also emerged during this period and significantly shaped our entertainment and cultural experiences. Nollywood movies became a staple in households nationwide, providing entertainment and a reflection of our society. The influence of Nollywood was so profound that it eventually became the second-largest film industry in the world.

Educational System

The educational system in Nigeria during the 90s and 2000s had its own set of challenges. While there were notable achievements, such as the increase in access to primary education and the establishment of more universities, there were also significant shortcomings. The quality of education varied greatly, with many schools lacking basic facilities and resources.

Furthermore, the system heavily emphasised rote learning and memorisation, leaving little room for critical thinking and creativity. Despite these challenges, many Nigerians excelled academically and pursued successful careers both within the country and abroad.

Economic Changes

Nigeria's economic landscape underwent significant changes during the 1990s and 2000s. In the 1990s, the country experienced a period of economic decline due to political instability and mismanagement of resources. This had a profound impact on Nigerians' lives, with widespread poverty and limited opportunities for economic growth.

However, Nigeria witnessed a gradual economic recovery towards the end of the 90s and into the 2000s. The country experienced increased foreign direct investment, particularly in telecommunications and oil. This led to the rise of mobile phone usage and improved internet access, transforming how we communicate and access information.

Impact on Identity

Growing up in Nigeria during the 90s and 2000s had a significant impact on our collective identity. It was a time of social and political awakening as we witnessed the transition from military rule to civilian democracy. This period also saw the emergence of a vibrant youth culture, with young

Nigerians actively participating in social and political movements.

The exposure to different cultures, both within Nigeria and from the rest of the world, also shaped our sense of identity. We became more aware of our heritage and the need to preserve our cultural traditions, while also embracing the influences of globalisation. This dynamic combination of local and global influences continues to shape the identity of young Nigerians today.

Growing up in Nigeria during the 90s and 2000s was a transformative experience that shaped the lives of many individuals. Cultural influences, educational systems, and economic changes all significantly shape our identities and aspirations. While there were challenges and obstacles to overcome, the resilience and determination of Nigerians allowed us to navigate through these changes and emerge stronger.

In conclusion, growing up in Nigeria during the 1990s and 2000s was a unique journey filled with diverse experiences. It was a time of cultural celebration, educational challenges, and economic transformations. The keyword phrase "Growing up in Nigeria (the 90s and 2000s)" encapsulates the essence of this period, highlighting its significance in shaping the lives of Nigerians.

Working with the Public Service

The Importance of Public Service

At this juncture, it is important to let you know that my maternal grandfather and mother were public servants. Thus, joining the public service has always weighed heavily on my mind from a tender age. Truth be told, I was not entirely sure about this, but when the time came, the transition was seamless. The public service plays a vital role in society, working towards the betterment of communities and ensuring the well-being of citizens. Working with the public service not only offers fulfilling career opportunities but also allows individuals to make a positive impact on society. Whether it is in government agencies, healthcare, education, or social work, working with the public service provides an avenue to serve the greater good.

Advantages of Working with the Public Service

Working with the public service offers several advantages that make it an attractive career choice for many individuals. Some of the advantages include:

- **Job Security:** Public service jobs often provide stable employment with consistent salaries and benefits, even during times of economic uncertainty. This level of job security can bring peace of mind and financial stability to individuals and their families.

- **Opportunities for Growth:** The public service sector provides ample opportunities for career advancement and growth. Employees can benefit from training programs, workshops, and educational opportunities to enhance their skills and knowledge. This allows individuals to progress in their careers and take on new challenges.

- **Sense of Purpose:** Working in public service gives individuals a sense of purpose as they contribute to the well-being of their communities. The work done in the public service directly impacts the lives of people, making a positive difference in society.
- **Diverse Work Environments:** The public service offers a wide range of career options across various sectors. Whether individuals prefer working in an office, in the field, or in a healthcare setting, there are opportunities available to suit different preferences and skill sets.
- **Collaborative Work:** Working with public service often involves collaborating with colleagues from different backgrounds and with different levels of expertise. This collaborative environment fosters teamwork and the exchange of ideas, leading to innovative solutions to societal challenges.

Challenges of Working with the Public Service

While working with the public service has many advantages, it also comes with its own set of challenges. Some of these challenges include:

- **Bureaucracy:** Public service organisations can sometimes be bureaucratic, with complex processes and hierarchies. Navigating through these structures can be time-consuming and requires patience and persistence.
- **High Expectations:** Public service employees often face high expectations from the public and stakeholders. Meeting these expectations and delivering quality services can sometimes be demanding and stressful.
- **Limited Resources:** Public service organisations often operate within limited budgets and resources. This can

pose challenges when trying to effectively meet the public's needs and demands.

- **Public Scrutiny:** Working in the public service means being under constant public scrutiny. Public servants' Decisions and actions are subject to public opinion and criticism, which can be challenging to navigate.

Working with the public service offered me the opportunity to contribute to the greater good and positively impact society. Despite the challenges that came with it, the advantages of working in the public service, such as job security, growth opportunities, and a sense of purpose, far outweighed the drawbacks. Whether it was through policymaking, social work, or healthcare services, the eight years I spent at the National Agency for the Control of AIDS (NACA) exposed me and helped hone my competencies across several areas of expertise. So, if you are passionate about working with the public service, seize the opportunity to make a difference and contribute to the betterment of our communities. Working with the public service is not just a job but a calling.

My Adventure in the International NGO Space

My adventure in the international NGO space has been a transformative journey that has allowed me to positively impact the lives of countless individuals around Africa, especially children. Working in this sector has broadened my horizons and given me a profound sense of purpose and fulfilment. On November 1st, 2021, I resumed as a Project Manager with eHealth Africa, and I must say, the lessons learned and growth have been phenomenal.

Embracing the Challenges

Working in the international NGO space, particularly across the African continent, presents its fair share of challenges. Every day, navigating different cultures and languages to address complex social issues brings a new set of hurdles to overcome. However, these challenges have fueled my passion and commitment to making a difference, especially for the African child. My personal mantra has always been "leave no child behind", and in our efforts to strengthen public health emergency management across the continent, I have immersed myself totally in the cause.

Key Learnings

Throughout my adventure, I have gained invaluable insights and skills that have shaped me personally and professionally. Some of the key learnings I have acquired include:

- The importance of cross-cultural communication and understanding proved critical to the success of the project in Somalia and Mozambique, where we had to adapt project implementation strategies to suit the prevailing socio-cultural norms.

- The power of collaboration and partnership in achieving sustainable change was instrumental in ensuring the success of the projects in Cameroun, Ethiopia, DR Congo, and Guinea Bissau.

- The need for innovative and adaptable solutions to address complex societal problems was critical to the success of the project in Mozambique, Madagascar, and DR Congo, where we had to overcome several constraints, particularly with regard to funds, scope, and time.

- Empathy and active listening are significant in building meaningful relationships, which formed the basis of successful project implementation in the 19 countries we were assigned.

- The role of advocacy and policy reform in creating long-term impact.

Making an Impact

One of the most rewarding aspects of my adventure in the international NGO space has been witnessing the tangible impact of our work. From providing access to improved data and tools through the Geographic Information Systems for improved immunisation campaigns to the setup of state-of-the-art public health infrastructure, particularly for underserved communities, every small step we take contributes to creating a brighter future for Africans in general and African children in particular.

Bold Steps Forward

It is essential to take bold steps to continue making a meaningful difference. This involves embracing innovation, leveraging technology, and adopting a proactive approach to addressing emerging challenges. By constantly pushing boundaries and thinking outside the box, we can amplify the impact of our efforts and create lasting change. This has been the mantra of the Program Delivery Team at eHealth Africa.

Passion is the driving force behind any successful endeavour, and the international NGO space is no exception. It is the passion for social justice and equality that fuels our determination to overcome obstacles and push for positive change. Without passion, our work would merely be a series of tasks, lacking the transformative power it possesses.

My adventure in the international NGO space has been an incredible journey, filled with numerous highs and lows. Through it all, my passion for making a difference has remained unwavering. The experiences, challenges, and learnings I have encountered have shaped me into a more empathetic, resilient, and effective changemaker.

As I reflect on my adventure in the international NGO space so far, I am filled with gratitude for the opportunities I have had and the lives I have been able to touch. It is through this work that I have further discovered my purpose and found fulfillment in making a positive impact on the world.

In conclusion, my adventure in the international NGO space has been a transformative and fulfilling experience that has allowed me to contribute to the betterment of society. The challenges I have faced, the learnings I have gained, and the impact I have made have shaped me into the changemaker I am today. My adventure in the international NGO space is far from over, and I am excited to continue making a difference in the lives of individuals around the world.

My Experience
Working Across Africa

Working across Africa has been an incredible journey filled with unique challenges, rewarding experiences, and unforgettable memories. Throughout my stint as Project Manager, I have had the opportunity to work in various countries across the continent, each offering its own set of opportunities and learnings. This chapter aims to share my firsthand experience and insights gained from working across Africa.

Embracing Diversity and Cultural Richness

One of the most remarkable aspects of working across Africa is the incredible diversity and cultural richness found within each country. From Somalia's fluid and fragile environment to Zimbabwe's rigid and structured delineation, DR Congo's dynamic and complex systems, to the calm of Brazzaville, every destination offers a unique blend of traditions, languages, and customs. This diversity not only enriches the experience but also presents an opportunity to learn and grow both personally and professionally.

Cultural Adaptability and Flexibility

Working across Africa has taught me the importance of cultural adaptability and flexibility. Each country has its own way of doing business, and understanding and respecting these cultural nuances is crucial for success. From the warm hospitality of West Africa to the precise timeliness of East Africa, adapting to local customs and practices is key to building strong relationships and fostering trust with colleagues and clients.

It is essential to embrace diversity, foster open-mindedness, and be willing to learn from different perspectives to thrive in a multicultural work environment. This flexibility not only allows for effective collaboration but also enhances problem-solving abilities and promotes innovation. These were crucial to the success of the project.

Overcoming Challenges

Working across Africa presents its fair share of challenges, but these obstacles have ultimately contributed to my personal and professional growth. The continent's vastness and diverse terrains can make logistics and travel challenging, requiring careful planning and adaptability. Moreover, infrastructure limitations, political instability, and economic disparities can complicate business operations.

However, by approaching these challenges with a positive mindset and a solution-oriented approach, I have successfully navigated them. These experiences have taught me resilience, problem-solving skills, and the ability to think independently – all valuable traits in any professional setting. Furthermore, they have contributed to the enrichment of my CV.

Building Strong Networks

One of the most valuable aspects of working across Africa is the opportunity to build strong networks with professionals from diverse backgrounds. The continent is home to a rich talent pool, and collaborating with individuals from different industries and sectors has broadened my perspective and expanded my professional network.

Building these networks requires active participation in industry events, conferences, and networking sessions.

Engaging in meaningful conversations, exchanging ideas, and seeking collaboration opportunities are important. These connections have not only opened doors for new business ventures but have also fostered lifelong friendships.

Promoting Sustainable Development

Working across Africa has also allowed me to contribute to sustainable development initiatives. The continent possesses immense potential for growth and progress, and it is crucial to harness this potential responsibly and sustainably. By working with local communities, NGOs, and government organisations, I have had the privilege of participating in projects that aim to positively impact society and the environment. Supporting healthcare initiatives has provided experiences that have reinforced my commitment to contributing to the sustainable development of the African continent.

The Future of Africa

On my first international trip as a project manager, I encountered a family on a flight from Addis Ababa to Dar es Salaam. This was a young family with two daughters, the older being about six years old. What intrigued me the most was the level of engagement between the father and elder daughter, with the young girl driving a mature and intelligent conversation with her dad. This reinforced my belief that Africa indeed has a bright future and that all that is needed is to provide our children with an enabling environment.

Reflecting on my experience working across Africa, I am optimistic about the continent's future. Africa has immense opportunity, with a young and dynamic population, abundant natural resources, and a growing middle class. The potential for economic growth and development is undeniable. However, realising this potential requires collaborative efforts from both local and international stakeholders. Infrastructure, education, healthcare, and technology investments are vital to unlocking Africa's full potential. Furthermore, fostering an environment that promotes entrepreneurship and innovation is crucial for sustainable economic growth.

In conclusion, my experience working across Africa has been nothing short of transformative. The continent's diversity, cultural richness, and growth potential have left an indelible mark on my professional journey. From overcoming challenges to building strong networks and contributing to sustainable development, Africa has provided me with invaluable experiences and learnings.

My experience working across Africa has shaped me into a more adaptable, resilient, and globally minded professional. I am grateful for my opportunities and remain optimistic about Africa's future. Through continued collaboration and investment, the continent will undoubtedly flourish and become a beacon of progress and innovation in the future.

The Centrality of Nigeria to Africa's Success

Nigeria, known as the "Giant of Africa," is a country of immense importance and influence. With a population of over 200 million, Nigeria's size alone makes it a crucial player in Africa's success. However, Nigeria's centrality goes beyond its population. The country's economy, political stability, and cultural influence contribute to its pivotal role in shaping Africa's future. Nigeria is the most populous country in Africa and plays a significant role in shaping the continent's development trajectory. With its vast resources, strategic location, and strong economic growth, Nigeria can potentially drive Africa's progress on multiple fronts. This chapter explores the key reasons Nigeria is central to Africa's development.

Economic Powerhouse

Nigeria boasts the largest economy in Africa, accounting for approximately 20% of the continent's GDP. The country is rich in natural resources, particularly oil, which has been a major driver of economic growth. Nigeria's oil reserves have positioned it as one of the world's top oil producers, allowing it to play a significant role in global energy markets.

Furthermore, Nigeria's economy extends beyond oil. The country has diverse sectors, including agriculture, telecommunications, banking, and entertainment. Its vibrant entrepreneurial spirit has led to a thriving tech industry, with Nigerian startups gaining domestic and international recognition. This economic diversity positions Nigeria as a potential hub for innovation and investment for Africa and the world.

Nigeria's Demographic Advantage

One of the primary reasons why Nigeria is central to Africa's development is its demographic advantage. With an estimated population of over 200 million, Nigeria represents a significant portion of Africa's total population. This large population can be harnessed to fuel economic growth and drive innovation. The sheer size of Nigeria's population provides a vast consumer market, attracting local and international businesses. This market potential creates opportunities for job creation, investment, and increased productivity, ultimately leading to developing industries and sectors that can benefit the entire continent.

Strategic Location and Connectivity

Nigeria's strategic location in West Africa positions it as a gateway to the rest of the continent. It shares borders with multiple countries, including Niger, Chad, Cameroon, and Benin Republic, making it a hub for regional trade and integration. Nigeria's ports, particularly Lagos, are major maritime gateways for goods entering and leaving West Africa. The country's connectivity through air transportation is also noteworthy, with several international airports serving as vital links between Africa and the rest of the world.

Abundance of Natural Resources

Nigeria is endowed with abundant natural resources, including oil, gas, minerals, and agricultural land. Its oil reserves make it one of the largest oil-producing countries in Africa and a major player in the global energy market. Revenue generated from oil exports can be channelled towards infrastructure development, education, healthcare, and other sectors crucial for Africa's progress. Nigeria's agricultural potential is immense, with fertile land and favourable climatic conditions. By harnessing its agricultural resources, Nigeria can contribute to food security within its borders and across the African continent.

Commitment to Regional Stability

Nigeria has demonstrated its commitment to regional stability by actively participating in peacekeeping missions and conflict resolution efforts across Africa. Nigeria is crucial in ensuring peace and security in conflict-prone regions and is a major contributor to the African Union's peacekeeping forces. Its leadership and involvement in regional organisations, such as the Economic Community of West African States (ECOWAS), further solidify Nigeria's central position in Africa's development. Stability and security are essential prerequisites for sustainable development, and Nigeria's contributions are invaluable.

Political Stability

Political stability is another crucial factor in Nigeria's centrality to Africa's success. While the country has faced its fair share of political challenges, including corruption and ethnic tensions, Nigeria has managed to maintain a relatively stable democracy since its return to civilian rule in 1999. This political stability is essential for attracting foreign investment, fostering economic growth, and ensuring regional security.

Additionally, Nigeria plays a significant role in regional peacekeeping efforts. The country has contributed troops to numerous United Nations and African Union missions, demonstrating its commitment to maintaining stability across the continent. Nigeria's involvement in peacekeeping operations highlights its responsibility as a regional power and its dedication to promoting African peace and security.

Cultural Influence

Nigeria's cultural influence stretches far beyond its borders. The country's music, film, and literature have gained international recognition and popularity. Nigerian musicians such as Fela Kuti, Burna Boy, and Wizkid have achieved global fame, contributing to the rise of Afrobeats as a genre. Nigerian movies, commonly called Nollywood, are the second-largest film industry in the world, surpassing Hollywood in terms of annual film productions. Nigerian authors, including Chinua Achebe and Chimamanda Ngozi Adichie, have contributed significantly to African literature.

This cultural influence allows Nigeria to shape the narrative of Africa, challenging stereotypes and showcasing the continent's artistic and creative talents. It provides a platform for African voices to be heard and appreciated globally. Nigeria's cultural contributions are a testament to its vibrant and diverse society, making it a cultural powerhouse on the African continent and beyond.

Key Contributions to Africa's Development

Nigeria's centrality to Africa's success can be further highlighted through its contributions to regional development initiatives. The country has played an active role in the African Union, working towards the continent's integration and development. Nigeria has been a key player in establishing regional economic communities, such as the Economic Community of West African States (ECOWAS). These organisations aim to promote economic cooperation, peace, and stability among member states, ultimately driving Africa's progress.

Furthermore, Nigeria has been at the forefront of regional infrastructure projects. The Trans-Saharan Highway, for example, is a key transportation route connecting the countries of West Africa to North Africa. Nigeria's involvement in such initiatives demonstrates its commitment to regional integration and connectivity, creating opportunities for trade, investment, and economic growth across Africa.

Conclusion

In conclusion, Nigeria's centrality to Africa's success cannot be overstated. The country's economic power, political stability, and cultural influence contribute to its pivotal role in shaping the continent's future. Nigeria's status as an economic powerhouse, commitment to political stability and regional peacekeeping efforts, cultural contributions, and active involvement in regional development initiatives all solidify its position as a central player in Africa's success.

Nigeria's potential as a catalyst for African progress is undeniable. As the country continues to grow and evolve, it must leverage its strengths to drive inclusive and sustainable development within its borders and across the entire continent. Nigeria's centrality to Africa's success cannot be underestimated, and it is crucial for Nigeria to seize the opportunities ahead and lead the way towards a prosperous and united Africa.

Political Elites or Neophytes?

Introduction

In the world of politics, a perennial debate revolves around the suitability of political elites versus neophytes for holding positions of power and influence. The term "political elites" refers to experienced individuals who have spent years in the political sphere, while "neophytes" are newcomers who lack extensive political experience. This chapter aims to explore the advantages and disadvantages of these two groups, highlighting the potential benefits and drawbacks they bring to the table, especially as it concerns Nigeria's political space.

The Case for Political Elites

Political elites have long been considered the backbone of established political systems. Here are some reasons why they are often favoured:

1. **Experience and Expertise**: Political elites have typically spent years immersed in governance, policymaking, and diplomacy intricacies. This experience equips them with a deep understanding of political dynamics and allows them to easily navigate complex issues.

2. **Established Networks**: Over time, political elites build extensive networks of contacts within the political arena. These connections can be valuable for negotiating and collaborating with other influential individuals and institutions, facilitating the smooth functioning of government.

3. **Policy Continuity**: Political elites are more likely to maintain a consistent policy agenda, as their experience and understanding of governance enable them to appreciate the long-term consequences of their decisions. This stability is often regarded as crucial for societal progress and predictability.

The Case for Neophytes

On the other hand, proponents of neophytes argue that fresh faces in politics can bring about much-needed change and innovation. Here are some reasons why neophytes are seen as valuable:

1. **Alternative Perspectives**: Neophytes often challenge the status quo and offer alternative viewpoints that political elites may have overlooked. Their outsider perspective can help identify and address issues that have been neglected or dismissed.

2. **Renewed Trust in Politics**: In many cases, political elites have become associated with corruption, scandals, or being out of touch with the general public's needs and aspirations. With their fresh approach, Neophytes can help reestablish trust in the political system and engage disillusioned citizens.

3. **Diverse Representation**: Neophytes often bring greater diversity to the political landscape regarding demographics and ideas. This diversity can lead to a more inclusive and representative government that considers the needs of a broader range of citizens.

Striking a Balance

While there are valid arguments for both political elites and neophytes, it is essential to strike a balance between the two. A healthy mix of experience and fresh perspectives can yield the best societal outcomes. Here are some ways to achieve this balance:

1. **Mentorship Programs**: Political elites can nurture and guide neophytes, sharing their knowledge and experience. This mentorship can help new entrants navigate the complex world of politics while avoiding common pitfalls.
2. **Term Limits**: Implementing term limits for political elites can ensure a regular infusion of new voices and ideas. This practice prevents stagnation and encourages a continuous renewal of leadership.
3. **Merit-based Selection**: Rather than solely relying on experience or popularity, a merit-based selection process can ensure that political elites and neophytes have an equal opportunity to contribute to governance. This approach values competence and expertise while allowing for fresh talent to emerge.

Conclusion

The debate between political elites and neophytes is generally nuanced, with valid arguments on both sides. Political elites bring experience, expertise, and established networks, ensuring policy continuity and stability. On the other hand, neophytes offer alternative perspectives, renewed trust in politics, and diverse representation. Balancing the two groups is crucial for a healthy and dynamic political system.

Ultimately, whether political elites or neophytes are more suitable for positions of power depends on the specific context and governance goals. A combination of experience, fresh perspectives, and merit-based selection processes can foster an inclusive and effective political landscape. By embracing the strengths of both groups, we can harness the potential of political elites and neophytes to build a better future for our societies.

In conclusion, the debate between political elites or neophytes continues to shape political discourse, challenging our understanding of leadership and governance. While political elites bring experience and stability, neophytes offer innovation and fresh perspectives. The key lies in finding the right balance and creating a system that values both the wisdom of experience and the enthusiasm of newcomers. This is what we must inculcate into our political selection process in Nigeria and Africa in general. It is time to start tapping into the vast and technically savvy human resource that abounds on the continent.

The Need for the Citizens to Engage More in the Political Space

Politics is an integral part of any democratic society, as it shapes the direction and policies of a nation. However, in recent times, there has been a decline in citizen engagement in the political space. Citizens must understand the significance of their involvement and actively participate in shaping the future of their country. The need for the citizens to engage more in the political space cannot be overstated.

Importance of Citizen Engagement

Citizen engagement in politics, particularly in Nigeria, is vital for several reasons. Here are some key points to consider:

1. **Representation**: A democracy thrives when all citizens are actively involved in decision-making. Engaging in politics ensures that policymakers represent and consider the diverse voices and perspectives of the citizens.

2. **Accountability**: When citizens actively participate in politics, they hold their elected officials accountable for their actions and decisions. This encourages transparency and reduces the likelihood of corruption and abuse of power.

3. **Policy Influence**: Citizens can influence policy decisions that align with their values and interests by engaging in the political space. It allows them to shape the direction of their country and work towards a society that reflects their aspirations.

4. **Social Change**: Politics is a powerful tool for driving social change. By actively participating in the political space, citizens can advocate for issues that matter to them, such as human rights, environmental protection, and social justice.

Barriers to Citizen Engagement

Despite the importance of citizen engagement, several barriers hinder active participation in the political space. These barriers include:

- **Lack of Information**: Many citizens are unaware of the political processes and how they can get involved. This lack of information hampers their ability to engage effectively.

- **Cynicism and Apathy**: Some citizens may feel disillusioned with politics due to corruption, partisan politics, or broken promises. This cynicism and apathy can discourage them from actively participating in the political space.

- **Time Constraints**: Busy schedules and other commitments can make it challenging for citizens to actively engage in politics.

Overcoming Barriers and Promoting Citizen Engagement

Several steps can be taken to address these barriers and promote citizen engagement:

1. **Education and Awareness**: Governments and organisations should focus on educating citizens about political processes, their rights, and the importance of their involvement. This can be done through school curricula, public campaigns, and community workshops.

2. **Transparency and Accountability**: Governments should strive to be transparent and accountable. This can help rebuild trust and encourage citizens to participate actively in the political space. In this sense, introducing electronic systems is critical to improving transparency. Upgrades to the electoral system, such as electronic voting, should be introduced, no matter the counterarguments. If Nigerians can send millions of Naira from their bank accounts via electronic transfers, there is no reason why they can't vote from the comfort of their homes and offices.

3. **Accessible Platforms**: Utilising technology to provide accessible platforms for citizen engagement can greatly enhance participation. Online platforms, mobile applications, and social media can be utilised to gather citizen input, opinions, and feedback.

4. **Incentives and Recognition**: Governments can offer incentives, such as tax breaks or recognition, to citizens who actively engage in politics. This can encourage more citizens to get involved and make a difference.

In conclusion, the need for citizens to engage more in the political space is crucial for the functioning of a healthy democracy. Citizen engagement promotes representation, accountability, policy influence, and social change. Despite the barriers, education, transparency, accessible platforms, and incentives can help overcome these challenges and encourage citizens to participate actively. Citizens must recognise their power and responsibility in shaping the future of their country. By engaging in the political space, citizens can ensure their voices are heard, and their interests are represented. The need for the citizens to engage more in the political space has never been more important.

Why the Youth is
Key to Development

The youth play a crucial role in the development of any society. They possess the energy, creativity, and potential to drive progress and positive change. In this chapter, we will explore why the youth is key to development and how investing in their education and empowerment can lead to a prosperous future.

The Power of the Nigerian Youth

1. **Energy and Enthusiasm:** The Nigerian youth are known for their boundless energy and enthusiasm. They are not burdened by the cynicism or complacency that can often hinder progress. Instead, they approach challenges with a fresh perspective and a can-do attitude.

2. **Creativity and Innovation:** Young Nigerians are natural innovators. They have a unique ability to think outside the box and generate new ideas and solutions. Their fresh perspective and willingness to take risks can lead to groundbreaking advancements in technology, science, and other fields.

3. **Technological Prowess:** Today's youth are digital natives, having grown up in the digital age. They have an innate understanding of technology and how to use it to their advantage, making them indispensable in the development of digital solutions and the adaptation of emerging technologies.

4. **Social Change Agents:** The youth are often at the forefront of social movements and activism. They have a

strong sense of justice and a desire to create a fairer, more equitable society. Their passion for social change can drive progress in human rights, environmental sustainability, and gender equality.

Investing in Youth Development

Investing in their education, skills development, and empowerment is crucial to harness the youth's potential and ensure sustainable development. Here are some key reasons why investing in youth development is essential:

Education as a Foundation

Education is the cornerstone of any society's progress. By investing in quality education for the youth, we equip them with the knowledge and skills necessary to thrive in an ever-evolving world. Accessible and inclusive education empowers young people to become active community participants and contribute to economic growth.

Unleashing Economic Potential

The youth are a valuable resource for economic growth. By providing them with opportunities for vocational training, entrepreneurship, and job creation, we can unleash their economic potential. Young entrepreneurs can drive innovation and create employment opportunities, contributing to the overall development of their communities.

Fostering Leadership and Civic Engagement

Investing in youth development nurtures future leaders. By providing platforms for youth participation in decision-making processes, we ensure their voices are heard, and their perspectives are considered. This fosters a sense of ownership and responsibility, empowering young people to become active citizens who can drive positive change in their communities.

Addressing Social and Environmental Challenges

The youth are passionate about creating a better world. Investing in their education and empowerment enables them to tackle pressing social and environmental challenges. Whether combating climate change, promoting sustainable development, or advocating for social justice, young people are at the forefront of these movements and can drive significant change.

The Role of Governments and Stakeholders

Realising the full potential of the youth requires the collective effort of governments, policymakers, and various stakeholders. Here are some key steps that can be taken to support youth development:

1. **Policy Frameworks:** Governments should create policies prioritising youth development and empowerment. These policies should focus on education, skills development, employment opportunities, and youth participation in decision-making processes.
2. **Investment in Education:** Adequate funding for education is crucial. Governments should invest in quality education accessible to all, regardless of socio-economic background. This includes providing scholarships, improving infrastructure, and enhancing the quality of teaching.
3. **Skills Development:** Governments and stakeholders should collaborate to provide vocational training programs, internships, and apprenticeships to equip the youth with the skills needed for the job market.

This will help bridge the gap between education and employment.

4. **Youth Engagement:** Governments should actively involve young people in decision-making processes at all levels. This can be done through youth councils, advisory boards, and platforms for youth participation in policy formulation and implementation.

5. **Entrepreneurship Support:** Governments and stakeholders should provide financial and technical support to young entrepreneurs. This can include access to capital, mentorship programs, and business development services to encourage entrepreneurship and innovation.

In conclusion, the youth is key to development due to their energy, creativity, and potential for positive change. Investing in their education, skills development, and empowerment can unlock their full potential and create a prosperous future. Governments and stakeholders must prioritise youth development and ensure their active participation in decision-making processes. Only by doing so can we fully leverage the power of the youth and drive sustainable growth. Why the youth is key to development is not just a statement but a reality we must embrace to shape a brighter future.

In the following three chapters, I will delve into some strategic sectors of the economy that can be easily deployed to harness the talents and energy of the Nigerian youth for national development. These sectors, often overlooked, serve as low-hanging fruits that can be quickly deployed to jumpstart Nigeria's journey of greatness.

Harnessing Sports for National Development

Sports have long been recognised as a form of entertainment and a powerful tool for national development. Harnessing sports' potential can lead to significant improvements in various aspects of a nation's development, including physical health, social cohesion, and economic growth. Harnessing sports for national development requires a strategic approach and investment in infrastructure, talent development, and community engagement.

The Impact of Sports on Physical Health

One of the sports' most obvious benefits is its positive impact on physical health. Regular participation in sports activities helps maintain a healthy weight, reduce the risk of chronic diseases, and promote overall fitness. Governments can actively combat the rising prevalence of sedentary lifestyles and related health issues by encouraging citizens to engage in sports.

Harnessing sports for national development entails investing in sports facilities, such as stadiums, gyms, and parks, that provide accessible spaces for people to engage in physical activities. Additionally, promoting school sports programs and community-based sports clubs can encourage young people to adopt an active lifestyle from an early age.

Infrastructure Investment

Investment in sports infrastructure is crucial in harnessing sports for national development. The availability of well-maintained sports facilities is essential to attract and facilitate sports events, competitions, and training programs. These facilities benefit professional athletes and provide recreational spaces for citizens of all ages and abilities.

Governments at all levels should prioritise the construction and maintenance of sports infrastructure, ensuring it is inclusive and accessible to all. This includes providing facilities catering to various sports disciplines, such as football, basketball, tennis, and swimming. By doing so, Nigeria can create an environment that nurtures talent and promotes a culture of physical activity. Furthermore, these infrastructures will galvanise talent development and management and provide gainful employment for people assigned to manage the infrastructure, simultaneously tackling the unemployment problem.

Talent Development

Harnessing sports for national development necessitates identifying and nurturing sporting talent. This involves creating pathways for aspiring athletes to receive proper training, coaching, and support. Developing a robust sports education system is crucial to identifying and grooming talented individuals who can represent their nation at national and international levels.

Investments in sports academies, coaching programs, and talent identification initiatives are essential to cultivate a pool of skilled trainers and athletes. Moreover, scholarships and financial incentives can motivate young athletes to pursue their dreams and excel in their chosen sports. By nurturing talent, Nigeria can elevate its sporting prowess and bring national pride through sporting achievements.

Consequently, investing in sports can be a strategic route to rejigging and galvanising Nigeria's education system. Furthermore, it can serve as a means of diversifying the economy as sport has proven to be a major driver of global finance, especially in the last 3-4 decades. By investing in talent development and exporting these talents to the world, Nigeria can benefit from the inflow of finances, and local sports clubs and academies will stand to gain.

In addition to the aforementioned, quality infrastructure and an abundance of sporting talent will greatly improve the commercial viability of our local sporting competitions across several categories. This has a knock-on effect on the economy, engendering economic prosperity and an improvement in the standard of living.

Social Cohesion and Integration

Sports have the unique power to unite people, transcending boundaries of race, religion, and socio-economic status. Harnessing sports for national development involves leveraging this power to foster social cohesion and integration within communities. Individuals from diverse backgrounds can come together through sports, work towards a common goal, and build lasting relationships.

Team sports, in particular, promote cooperation, teamwork, and mutual respect among players. Sporting events and competitions allow individuals to interact and understand different cultures, breaking societal barriers. By organising inclusive sports programs and events, Nigeria can create a sense of unity and pride among their citizens. For instance, sporting events such as the Principal's Cup, NUGA, NIPOGA and others, to mention a few, can strengthen integration in Nigeria. It is, therefore, a shame that the government, especially at the federal level, has treated sports with so much disdain, overlooking its latent benefits and immense socio-economic potential.

Community Engagement

Community engagement is a key aspect of harnessing sports for national development. It actively involves citizens and local communities in sports activities and initiatives. By encouraging grassroots participation, governments can ensure that sports' benefits extend to all segments of society.

Community sports programs, such as neighbourhood leagues and inter-school competitions, allow individuals of all ages to engage in sports. These programs promote physical health, build social connections, and a sense of belonging. By investing in community sports infrastructure and organising inclusive events, nations can empower their citizens and promote active citizenship.

Economic Growth and Tourism

Harnessing sports for national development goes beyond physical and social benefits. Sports can also significantly impact a nation's economy by fostering tourism, generating employment opportunities, and boosting the sports industry.

Hosting international sporting events, such as the Olympics or World Cup, can attract tourists worldwide, resulting in increased revenue for the host country. Moreover, developing sports-related industries, such as sports manufacturing, tourism, and media, can create jobs and contribute to economic growth.

By leveraging the potential of sports, Nigeria can tap into the economic opportunities that arise from hosting sporting events, attracting tourists, and developing sports-related industries. This stimulates economic growth and enhances the country's international reputation and standing.

In conclusion, harnessing sports for national development is a multi-faceted endeavour that requires a comprehensive approach. Investment in sports infrastructure, talent development, and community engagement can positively impact physical health, social cohesion, and economic growth. By recognising and utilising the power of sports, nations can truly harness sports for national development, benefiting their citizens and fostering a sense of national pride and unity. Harnessing Sports for National Development is a catchphrase and a strategic pathway towards a brighter future. Thus, nominees for the Minister/Commissioner for youth and sports should be seasoned, passionate and knowledgeable professionals who will galvanise this sector of the country's economy.

Harnessing Tech for National Development

Technology has become an indispensable tool in today's world. Rapid advancements in technology have transformed every aspect of our lives, from communication to transportation and education to healthcare. Harnessing technology for national development is crucial for countries to stay competitive and thrive in the global economy. This chapter explores the various ways technology can be utilised to drive national development and create a prosperous future.

The Role of Technology in National Development

Technology can revolutionise economies, improve governance, and enhance the quality of life for citizens. We have witnessed this across the world. By harnessing tech for national development, Nigeria can achieve sustainable growth, increase productivity, and create employment opportunities. Here are some key areas where technology can make a significant impact on Nigeria's economy:

Education: Technology has transformed the way knowledge is imparted and acquired. With the advent of online learning platforms, students can access educational resources from anywhere in the world. E-learning has not only made education more accessible but also personalised, allowing students to learn at their own pace. Virtual reality (VR) and augmented reality (AR) technologies are also being integrated into classrooms, providing immersive and interactive learning experiences. Harnessing tech for national development in education is essential to ensure that the future workforce is equipped with the necessary skills and knowledge.

Healthcare: The healthcare sector has greatly benefited from technological advancements. Technology has transformed how healthcare services are delivered, from telemedicine to electronic health records. Telemedicine enables patients in remote areas to access quality healthcare without needing physical travel. Electronic health records have made it easier for healthcare providers to access and share patient information, leading to more efficient and accurate diagnoses. Artificial intelligence (AI) in healthcare is also on the rise, with AI-powered algorithms being used to analyse medical images and predict disease outcomes. Harnessing tech for national development in healthcare can lead to better healthcare outcomes, improved patient experiences, and cost savings. Recently, I saw a video of surgeons in the UK operating on a banana using 5G technology. These and many more are the offerings technology has for improved healthcare.

Infrastructure Development

Technology plays a vital role in building sustainable and resilient infrastructure. The Internet of Things (IoT) enables the monitoring and managing of critical infrastructure such as bridges, roads, and power grids. Smart cities leverage technology to optimise energy consumption, enhance transportation systems, and improve public safety. Renewable energy technologies like solar and wind power are also crucial for sustainable infrastructure development. By harnessing tech for national development in infrastructure, countries can create more efficient and eco-friendly cities, improve connectivity, and ensure the well-being of their citizens.

Agriculture: Agriculture is the backbone of many economies, especially in developing countries. Technology can significantly increase agricultural productivity, improve food security, and reduce environmental impact. Precision farming techniques, such as using drones for crop monitoring and data analytics to optimise irrigation and fertilisation, can help farmers make informed decisions and maximise yields. Mobile applications and online platforms can connect farmers with markets, enabling them to sell their produce fairly. Harnessing tech for national agricultural development can lead to increased food production, rural development, and poverty reduction.

Governance and Public Services

Technology can revolutionise governance and public services, making them more transparent, efficient, and citizen-centric. E-government initiatives aim to digitise government processes, making them accessible online and reducing bureaucracy. Online citizen engagement and feedback platforms can enable governments to make more informed policy decisions and improve public service delivery. Blockchain technology can potentially enhance transparency and security in voting, identity management, and public procurement. Harnessing tech for national development in governance can lead to more accountable and responsive governments, fostering trust and confidence among citizens.

Conclusion

Harnessing tech for national development is vital for countries to thrive in the digital age. Countries can unlock their full potential and achieve sustainable growth by leveraging technology in education, healthcare, infrastructure development, agriculture, and governance. However, it is essential to ensure that technology is accessible to all citizens, bridging the digital divide and leaving no one behind. Governments, private sector organisations, and civil society must work together to create an enabling environment for technological innovation and ensure all share its benefits. Only by embracing technology can Nigeria harness its power for national development and create a prosperous future for its citizens.

Harnessing the Creative Industry for National Development

The creative industry has emerged as a powerful force driving economic growth and development in nations worldwide. From art and design to film and music, this sector has the potential to stimulate innovation, create jobs, and enhance a nation's overall well-being. Harnessing the creative industry for national development is essential for countries looking to diversify their economies, attract investment, and foster cultural enrichment. This chapter explores the importance of this industry and highlights strategies to maximise its potential.

The Power of the Creative Industry

The creative industry encompasses various sectors, including visual arts, performing arts, media, advertising, and design. It is a dynamic and rapidly expanding sector that thrives on imagination, innovation, and talent. This industry contributes to economic growth and plays a significant role in shaping national identity and cultural heritage.

Economic Growth and Job Creation

The creative industry has proven to be a valuable contributor to economic growth. According to a report by the United Nations Conference on Trade and Development (UNCTAD), the creative economy's global market value reached $2.25 trillion in 2019. This figure is expected to grow further as countries recognise the potential of their creative sectors.

By investing in the creative industry, countries can create new employment opportunities and reduce unemployment rates. The industry employs diverse professionals, including artists, designers, musicians, filmmakers, and technicians. These jobs not only provide financial stability but also foster creativity and self-expression.

Innovation and Technological Advancement

The creative industry is at the forefront of innovation and technological advancement. It continually pushes the boundaries of what is possible, driving advancements in various fields. For instance, the film industry has played a crucial role in the development of visual effects and computer-generated imagery (CGI) techniques, which have been widely adopted in other industries, such as architecture and engineering.

Moreover, the creative industry thrives on collaboration and interdisciplinary work. Artists and designers often collaborate with scientists, engineers, and technologists to develop cutting-edge solutions and products. This cross-pollination of ideas fosters innovation and drives progress.

Cultural Enrichment and National Identity

The creative industry in Nigeria, particularly Nollywood, is a powerful tool for preserving and promoting cultural heritage. It serves as a platform for artists to express their unique perspectives, traditions, and values. Nigeria can preserve its cultural identity and promote diversity by supporting and showcasing local talent.

Furthermore, the creative industry plays a vital role in attracting tourists and visitors, contributing to the growth of the tourism sector. Cultural festivals, art exhibitions, and music events draw international attention, generating revenue and promoting local businesses.

Strategies to Harness the Creative Industry

Countries must adopt a holistic approach to harness the creative industry's potential for national development. Here are some strategies to consider:

- **Investment in Education and Training:** Nurturing creative talent starts with providing quality education and training programs. Governments should collaborate with educational institutions and industry experts to develop comprehensive curricula that equip students with the necessary skills and knowledge.
- **Infrastructure Development:** The creative industry relies heavily on infrastructure, such as art galleries, performance venues, and production studios. Governments should facilitate investment in constructing and maintaining these facilities to provide artists and creative professionals with the necessary resources.
- **Financial Support and Incentives:** Governments can provide financial support and incentives to attract investments in the creative industry. Grants, tax breaks, and subsidies encourage entrepreneurs and investors to establish creative businesses and initiatives.
- **Promotion of Collaboration and Networking:** Creating platforms for collaboration and networking is crucial for the growth of the creative industry. Governments can organise industry-specific events, conferences, and workshops to facilitate interactions between artists, designers, and potential collaborators.
- **International Partnerships:** Collaborating with international partners can provide access to global markets, expertise, and funding opportunities.

Governments should actively seek partnerships with other countries to promote their creative industries globally.

Nigeria can leverage the creative industry's potential to drive national development and economic growth by implementing these strategies.

In conclusion, harnessing the creative industry for national development is essential, particularly for a country like Nigeria looking to diversify its economy, create employment opportunities, and preserve its cultural heritage. This dynamic sector has the power to stimulate innovation, drive technological advancements, and attract investment, as is already being witnessed. However, more can be harnessed by investing in education, infrastructure, and financial support, thereby unleashing the full potential of the creative industries. Embracing collaboration, networking, and international partnerships will enhance the industry's impact. Therefore, governments must recognise the significance of harnessing the creative sector for national development and take proactive measures to support its growth and prosperity. In my travels to some African countries, I witnessed first-hand the significant influence Nigeria's movie and music industries have. The country can reap more rewards with coordinated strategies to strengthen this sector.

How the Education Sector Supports Every Other Sector of the Economy

The education sector plays a crucial role in supporting and shaping every other sector of the economy. It is the foundation upon which a skilled and knowledgeable workforce is built, contributing to the growth and development of industries. From the early years of schooling to higher education and vocational training, the education sector provides individuals with the necessary skills, knowledge, and capabilities to thrive in various professions. This chapter will explore how the education sector supports and impacts other sectors of the economy.

Importance of Education for Economic Growth

Education is often referred to as the engine of economic growth. It equips individuals with the skills and knowledge needed to succeed in the workforce, driving productivity and innovation across industries. A well-educated population is more likely to secure higher-paying jobs and contribute significantly to economic development. Studies have consistently shown a positive correlation between education levels and economic growth.

Enhancing Human Capital

The education sector enhances human capital by developing a skilled and knowledgeable workforce. Providing quality education to students equips them with the necessary skills to meet the demands of the job market. This, in turn, benefits various sectors of the economy by ensuring a pool of qualified workers. Industries such as technology, healthcare, engineering, and finance heavily rely on highly skilled professionals who have received a quality education.

Meeting Industry Demands

As industries evolve and grow, the education sector plays a crucial role in meeting their changing demands. By aligning curricula with industry needs and trends, educational institutions ensure that students are equipped with the skills and knowledge required in the job market. This collaboration between the education sector and industries helps bridge the gap between academic knowledge and practical skills, making graduates more employable and adaptable to industry changes.

Research and Innovation

The education sector also contributes to research and innovation, which are vital for the growth of various sectors of the economy. Universities and research institutions conduct groundbreaking research, leading to discoveries and advancements in medicine, technology, and renewable energy. The knowledge generated through research helps spur innovation, driving economic growth and competitiveness. Moreover, educational institutions often collaborate with industries to develop innovative solutions to real-world problems.

Entrepreneurship and Start-ups

Education fosters an entrepreneurial mindset and encourages the creation of start-ups. By providing students with the necessary knowledge and skills to start their businesses, the education sector contributes to the growth of the entrepreneurial ecosystem. Start-ups and small businesses are significant in job creation, innovation, and economic development. The education sector supports entrepreneurship by offering courses and programs that teach entrepreneurial skills, providing mentorship and guidance, and facilitating access to resources and networks.

Economic Mobility and Social Equality

Education is a powerful tool for promoting economic mobility and reducing social inequality. It gives individuals from all backgrounds equal opportunity to acquire knowledge and skills, regardless of their socioeconomic status. By providing accessible and affordable education, the education sector helps level the playing field, enabling individuals to break the cycle of poverty and achieve upward social mobility. This, in turn, benefits the economy by creating a more diverse and skilled workforce.

Global Competitiveness

A competitive economy relies on a well-educated workforce in an increasingly globalised world. The education sector plays a vital role in ensuring that individuals are globally competitive. By offering international programs, language learning opportunities, and cultural exchanges, educational institutions prepare students to thrive in a global marketplace. This global outlook enhances the competitiveness of various sectors, such as international trade, tourism, and technology, contributing to economic growth and prosperity.

Conclusion

In conclusion, the education sector is the backbone of every other sector of the economy. It plays a pivotal role in supporting economic growth, enhancing human capital, meeting industry demands, fostering research and innovation, promoting entrepreneurship, reducing social inequality, and ensuring global competitiveness. The education sector equips individuals with the skills and knowledge needed for success in the workforce, driving productivity, innovation, and economic development. The way the education sector supports every other sector of the economy cannot be overstated. Its impact is far-reaching and essential for nations' prosperity and individuals' well-being

.

It is a fundamental aspect that cannot be overlooked: how education supports every other sector of the economy. The sector's contributions are invaluable in shaping the economic landscape and driving growth. By investing in education, Nigeria can secure a prosperous and sustainable future.

The Need to Recalibrate the Education System

Introduction

The education system plays a crucial role in shaping the future of individuals and societies. However, in today's rapidly changing world, there is an urgent need to recalibrate the education system in Nigeria to ensure it remains relevant and effective. This has become a pressing issue due to various factors, such as technological advancements, evolving job market demands, and changing societal needs.

Adapting to Technological Advancements

One of the primary reasons for recalibrating the education system is the rapid advancement of technology. The digital revolution has transformed how we live, work, and communicate. However, our education system must often catch up with these technological changes. As a result, students are not adequately prepared for the digital world they will face upon graduation.

Schools need to integrate technology into their curriculum early to address this issue. Students should be taught essential digital skills such as coding, data analysis, and critical thinking. By incorporating technology into education, we can equip students with the necessary tools to thrive in the digital era.

Meeting Evolving Job Market Demands

The job market constantly evolves, and the education system must adapt accordingly. Many traditional jobs are being automated or outsourced, while new fields such as artificial intelligence and renewable energy are emerging. To ensure students are prepared for future jobs, the education system needs to focus on developing transferable skills.

Instead of emphasising rote memorisation, the education system should prioritise critical thinking, problem-solving, creativity, and collaboration. These skills are essential for success in the modern workplace, where adaptability and innovation are highly valued. We can bridge the gap between education and employment by recalibrating the education system to prioritise these skills.

Addressing Changing Societal Needs

Societies are constantly evolving, and the education system should reflect these changes. Today's students are growing up in a diverse and interconnected world, facing challenges such as climate change, social inequality, and global conflicts. The education system needs to incorporate a broader range of subjects and perspectives to prepare them for these challenges.

Subjects like environmental studies, ethics, and global citizenship should be integrated into the curriculum. This will help students develop a holistic understanding of the world and become responsible global citizens. By recalibrating the education system to address changing societal needs, we can empower students to make a positive impact on their communities and the world at large.

Conclusion

In conclusion, the need to recalibrate Nigeria's education system has become increasingly evident in today's rapidly changing world. Technological advancements, evolving job market demands, and changing societal needs all necessitate a shift in how we educate our children. By integrating technology, focusing on transferable skills, and addressing societal challenges, we can ensure our education system remains relevant and effective, producing a workforce that is fit for purpose.

It is, therefore, crucial for policymakers, educators, and stakeholders to come together and prioritise the need to recalibrate the education system. Only by doing so can we equip our students with the skills and knowledge they need to thrive in the 21st century. The need to recalibrate the education system cannot be ignored if we want to prepare the next generation for the challenges and opportunities that lie ahead, particularly if we want to give them a fighting chance in this ever-demanding and competitive world.

Harnessing Nigeria's Cultural Diversity for Development

Nigeria, with its vast array of ethnic groups and languages, is a country rich in cultural diversity. This diversity is not only a source of pride but also a potential catalyst for development. Harnessing Nigeria's cultural diversity for development can bring about economic prosperity, social cohesion, and sustainable growth. By recognising and embracing the unique strengths of each culture, Nigeria can unlock its full potential and create a thriving nation.

Embracing Cultural Diversity

Nigeria is home to over 250 ethnic groups, each with its own distinct culture, traditions, and languages. This cultural diversity is a testament to the richness of the Nigerian identity. It is essential to recognise and embrace this diversity as a valuable resource for development. By celebrating and preserving traditional practices, languages, and customs, Nigeria can foster a sense of pride and unity among its citizens.

Economic Opportunities

Harnessing Nigeria's cultural diversity can open up numerous economic opportunities. Traditional crafts, arts, and cultural practices can be harnessed and transformed into viable industries. For example, Nigeria's vibrant music and film industries have gained international recognition, contributing significantly to the country's economy. By investing in cultural tourism and promoting indigenous products, Nigeria can attract local and international visitors, boost revenue, and create jobs.

Moreover, cultural diversity can foster innovation and creativity. Different perspectives and approaches brought about by diverse cultures can lead to the development of unique solutions to societal challenges. By promoting collaboration and exchange of ideas between different ethnic groups, Nigeria can tap into its diverse population's collective knowledge and expertise.

Social Cohesion and Unity

Harnessing Nigeria's cultural diversity is not only beneficial for economic development but also crucial for fostering social cohesion and unity. Embracing diversity promotes a sense of inclusion and acceptance among different ethnic groups. By encouraging cultural exchange and interaction, Nigeria can break down barriers and build bridges between communities, fostering mutual understanding and respect.

Furthermore, celebrating cultural diversity can help address issues of discrimination and prejudice. Nigeria can challenge negative stereotypes and promote tolerance and acceptance by promoting cultural education and awareness. This will contribute to a more harmonious and inclusive society where every citizen feels valued and respected.

Preserving Cultural Heritage

Preserving Nigeria's cultural heritage is vital for harnessing its diversity for development. Traditional practices, languages, and customs hold historical and cultural significance that should be safeguarded for future generations. Efforts should be made to document and protect indigenous knowledge systems, ensuring their transmission to younger generations.

Investing in cultural infrastructure, such as museums and cultural centres, can provide spaces for showcasing and preserving Nigeria's diverse cultural heritage. These spaces can serve as educational resources for both locals and tourists, fostering a deeper understanding and appreciation of Nigeria's rich cultural tapestry.

Government Support and Policies

The Nigerian government plays a crucial role in harnessing cultural diversity for development. Policies should be put in place to promote and protect cultural diversity and provide support to cultural industries. This can include financial incentives, grants, and training programs to encourage the growth of cultural enterprises.

Education also plays a vital role in promoting cultural diversity. Incorporating cultural diversity into the national curriculum can foster a sense of pride in one's culture and respect for others. By teaching children about Nigeria's diverse cultural heritage, future generations will appreciate the country's rich tapestry of cultures.

Conclusion

Harnessing Nigeria's cultural diversity for development is a powerful tool that can lead to economic prosperity, social cohesion, and sustainable growth. By embracing and celebrating cultural diversity, Nigeria can unlock its full potential and create a more inclusive and prosperous nation.

Nigeria must recognise the value of its diverse ethnic groups and languages and promote collaboration and the exchange of ideas between them. By investing in cultural industries, preserving cultural heritage, and implementing supportive policies, Nigeria can truly harness its cultural diversity for development. The future of Nigeria lies in the hands of its diverse population, united in the pursuit of development and progress.

The Role of the Public Service in National Development

Introduction

The role of public service in national development is crucial to ensuring the effective functioning of a country's government and the nation's overall progress. Public service refers to the individuals and organisations employed by the government to provide essential services and implement policies that contribute to the well-being of the citizens. This chapter will explore the significance of the public service in national development and highlight its key responsibilities.

Key Responsibilities of the Public Service

The public service plays a multifaceted role in promoting national development. Some of its key responsibilities include:

1. **Policy Formulation and Implementation**: The public service is responsible for formulating policies that address the nation's needs and challenges. These policies are developed based on extensive research, data analysis, and consultations with relevant stakeholders. Once the policies are formulated, the public service coordinates with various government departments and agencies to ensure effective implementation.

2. **Service Delivery**: The public service is responsible for delivering essential services to the citizens. This includes sectors such as healthcare, education, infrastructure development, social welfare, and public safety. By

ensuring the provision of quality services, the public service contributes to the overall well-being and development of the nation.

3. **Regulation and Enforcement**: The public service plays a crucial role in regulating various sectors of the economy to ensure fair competition and protect the interests of the citizens. It develops and enforces regulations and standards that govern industries, businesses, and public institutions. This helps create a conducive environment for economic growth and protects consumers from exploitation.

4. **Public Administration**: The public service is responsible for the efficient and effective administration of government operations. It manages the day-to-day functioning of government departments, oversees the allocation of resources, and ensures adherence to legal and ethical standards. By promoting good governance and accountability, the public service contributes to the nation's overall development.

Importance of the Public Service in National Development

The role of the public service in national development cannot be overstated. It serves as the backbone of the government and plays a vital role in shaping the future of a country. Here are some reasons why the public service is important:

1. **Policy Expertise**: The public service comprises professionals with diverse expertise and skills. These individuals possess in-depth knowledge of various sectors and are equipped to develop and implement policies that address complex social, economic, and political issues. Their expertise ensures that policies are evidence-based, practical, and aligned with the nation's long-term development goals.

2. **Efficient Service Delivery**: The public service is responsible for ensuring the efficient and equitable delivery of public services. By streamlining processes, improving service quality, and adopting innovative approaches, the public service enhances citizens' overall experience. This improves the standard of living and fosters a sense of trust and confidence in the government.

3. **Public Accountability**: The public service is crucial in upholding public accountability. It ensures that government resources are utilised judiciously and in the best interest of the citizens. Through effective monitoring and evaluation mechanisms, the public service identifies areas for improvement and takes corrective actions to enhance the efficiency and effectiveness of government programs.

4. **Stability and Continuity**: The public service provides stability and continuity in governance. Regardless of changes in political leadership, the public service remains steadfast in its commitment to serving the nation. This ensures the smooth functioning of government operations and the implementation of long-term development plans.

From the foregoing, it therefore beggars belief that successive administrations have treated Nigeria's public service as a means of recompensing political favours for individuals and ethnicities. Truth be told, any serious-minded society treats its public service with respect and utmost professionalism, but the reverse is the case with Nigeria. This is not to say that the service is entirely bad, as some of the most brilliant minds in the world are domiciled in Nigeria's public service. The challenge is that the few good ones are overburdened with the task of not just fulfilling their responsibilities but also those of others whose skills are not congruent with the responsibilities saddled them.

Conclusion

In conclusion, the role of the public service in national development is of utmost importance. It is responsible for policy formulation and implementation, service delivery, regulation and enforcement, and public administration. The public service contributes to the nation's overall progress by providing policy expertise, ensuring efficient service delivery, upholding public accountability, and providing stability and continuity in governance. The role of the public service in national development cannot be underestimated, as it lays the foundation for a prosperous and inclusive society. Therefore, governments must invest in the development and capacity-building of their public service to ensure sustained national growth and development.

Overall, the public service's role in national development is vital in shaping a country's future and ensuring the well-being of its citizens. The public service plays a crucial role in policy formulation, service delivery, regulation, and public administration. By fulfilling its responsibilities effectively, the public service contributes to the overall progress and development of the nation. The role of public service in national development must be recognised and supported by governments worldwide.

Based on the foregoing, it is expedient to reform Nigeria's public service. Here are some recommendations:

1. Implementation of a minimum wage that covers the needs of workers.
2. Digitisation and digitalisation of the public service to improve efficiency and transparency.
3. A concerted effort to attract the best minds from our tertiary institutions into the service.

4. Re-sizing the public service into a lean and mean entity. In this regard, Government-owned Enterprises should be streamlined to eliminate duplication of responsibilities. Also, government employees should be appropriately assessed to determine ministries, departments and agencies that best fit their competencies.

The Case for a Lean and Mean Public Service

In today's fast-paced world, efficiency and effectiveness have become crucial for any organisation to thrive. The public service sector is no exception to this rule. A lean and mean public service is vital for governments to meet the needs of their citizens while optimising the use of taxpayer Naira. This chapter will explore the benefits of a lean and mean public service, highlighting how it can lead to better outcomes and increased public trust.

What Does It Mean to Be Lean and Mean?

A lean public service refers to an organisation that operates with a focus on efficiency, effectiveness, and fiscal responsibility. It entails streamlining processes, eliminating waste, and maximising the use of available resources. By adopting this approach, public service organisations can provide high-quality services while minimising costs and bureaucracy.

The Benefits of a Lean and Mean Public Service

Implementing a lean and mean public service model offers several advantages that can positively impact the government and its citizens. Some of these benefits include:

- **Cost Savings**: A lean and mean public service can significantly reduce costs by eliminating unnecessary bureaucracy and streamlining processes. This allows governments to allocate resources to other critical areas such as healthcare, education, and infrastructure.

- **Improved Service Delivery**: A lean and mean public service focuses on delivering services efficiently and effectively. By cutting unnecessary red tape and bureaucracy, citizens can receive the assistance they need promptly. This leads to increased satisfaction and trust in the government's ability to meet their needs.

- **Increased Transparency**: Lean and mean public service organisations often emphasise transparency and accountability. By reducing unnecessary layers of bureaucracy, decision-making processes become more transparent, making it easier for citizens to understand how and why government decisions are made.

- **Enhanced Employee Morale**: A lean and mean public service encourages a culture of continuous improvement and innovation. Empowering employees to identify and eliminate waste increases their engagement and motivation, which in turn leads to higher productivity and job satisfaction.

- **Adaptability and Responsiveness**: Lean and mean public service organisations are better equipped to adapt to changing circumstances and respond to emergencies. By eliminating unnecessary layers of bureaucracy, decision-making becomes faster and more agile, allowing governments to address urgent issues promptly.

Overcoming Challenges in Implementing a Lean and Mean Public Service

While the benefits of a lean and mean public service are undeniable, implementing such a model will face some challenges. These challenges can include resistance to change, bureaucratic inertia, and public servants' fear of job losses. However, with effective leadership, clear communication, and a focus on upskilling and reskilling employees, these challenges can be overcome.

Public service organisations can provide training programs and resources to help employees develop new skills and adapt to the changing demands of a lean and mean environment. Governments at all levels can ensure a smooth transition to a lean and mean public service by investing in their workforce.

Real-World Examples

Several countries have successfully implemented a lean and mean public service model, reaping the benefits of increased efficiency and effectiveness. For example, the Government of New Zealand adopted a lean and mean approach to transform its public service. Through initiatives such as the Better Public Services program, the government focused on reducing bureaucracy, increasing transparency, and delivering better citizen outcomes.

Similarly, Singapore has been recognised for its lean and mean public service. The country's Civil Service College provides training programs to equip public service employees with the necessary skills to deliver high-quality services efficiently.

Conclusion

In conclusion, Nigeria's case for a lean and mean public service is compelling. By embracing efficiency, effectiveness, and fiscal responsibility, governments can provide better services to their citizens while optimising taxpayer dollars. A lean and mean public service leads to cost savings, improved service delivery, increased transparency, enhanced employee morale, and adaptability. Despite the challenges, the benefits of a lean and mean public service can be realised with effective leadership and a focus on upskilling employees.

In today's rapidly changing world, the need for a lean and mean public service has never been more critical. It is time for Nigeria to prioritise efficiency and effectiveness to meet the evolving needs of its citizens. By embracing a lean and mean approach, governments can build public trust, deliver better outcomes, and pave the way for a brighter future.

The case for a lean and mean public service is not just a concept; it is a necessity for the success of governments worldwide.

Why Equity and Fairness Is Critical to National Cohesion and Development

National cohesion and development are essential pillars for any country's progress and stability. To achieve these goals, it is imperative to prioritise equity and fairness in all aspects of society. Equity and fairness ensure that all individuals have equal opportunities and are treated justly, regardless of their background or circumstances. This chapter explores the significance of equity and fairness in fostering national cohesion and driving sustainable development.

The Meaning of Equity and Fairness

Before delving into the importance of equity and fairness, it is crucial to understand their meanings. Equity refers to the concept of providing individuals with the resources and support they need to thrive, taking into account their unique circumstances and challenges. Fairness, on the other hand, emphasises treating people impartially and justly, without discrimination or favouritism.

The Role of Equity and Fairness in Society

Equity and fairness are pivotal in achieving social justice and societal harmony. When individuals feel that they are being treated fairly and have equal opportunities, they are more likely to be engaged and motivated to contribute to the betterment of their nation. On the contrary, when there is a lack of equity and fairness, it can lead to deep divisions and resentment within society, hindering progress and development.

To further emphasise the significance of equity and fairness, here are some key points:

- **Equal Access to Education**: Equitable access to quality education ensures that all individuals, regardless of their socio-economic background or geographical location, can acquire knowledge and skills. This empowers individuals to contribute to the development of their country and reduces inequality.

- **Economic Stability and Inclusivity**: Fair economic policies that promote equal opportunities for all citizens foster economic stability and inclusivity. This results in reduced poverty rates, increased productivity, and a stronger economy. When individuals feel they have a fair chance to succeed, they are more likely to actively participate in the workforce actively, leading to greater national development.

- **Social Cohesion and Harmony**: Equity and fairness are vital for building social cohesion and harmony within a nation. When individuals perceive that they are being treated fairly and have access to equal opportunities, it fosters trust and solidarity among different segments of society. This unity is crucial for addressing social issues, resolving conflicts, and working together towards common goals.

- **Political Stability and Good Governance**: Countries prioritising equity and fairness are likelier to have political stability and good governance. Fair and transparent political processes ensure that all citizens have an equal say in decision-making, reducing tension and promoting peaceful coexistence. Furthermore, equitable distribution of resources and services strengthens citizens' trust in the government, leading to effective governance and sustainable development.

- In conclusion, the importance of equity and fairness in achieving national cohesion and development cannot be overstated. When individuals are treated equitably and fairly, it creates a sense of belonging and unity within society. This inclusivity and cohesion drive progress, innovation, and sustainable development. Therefore, the Nigerian government and policymakers must prioritise equity and fairness in their policies and practices. By doing so, they can create a more just and prosperous nation for all its citizens.

Why equity and fairness is critical to national cohesion and development is a concept that should guide every aspect of society. By promoting equality and justice, Nigeria can foster social cohesion, economic stability, and political harmony. Governments and individuals alike need to recognise the significance of equity and fairness in shaping a prosperous and cohesive nation.

Corruption Is a Symptom,
Not a Root Cause

Introduction

Corruption is a widespread issue that plagues societies around the world. It manifests in various forms, such as bribery, embezzlement, nepotism, and fraud. Many perceive corruption as the root cause of economic and social problems in a country. However, upon closer examination, it becomes evident that corruption is merely a symptom of deeper underlying issues. This chapter highlights that corruption is not the root cause but rather a consequence of systemic failures and societal shortcomings.

Understanding Corruption as a Symptom

1. Corruption As a Reflection of Social Norms

Corruption often reflects a society's prevailing social norms. In some cultures, practices such as favouritism and nepotism are deeply ingrained, leading to corruption as individuals exploit their positions of power for personal gain. These social norms may have historical roots or be perpetuated by the absence of strong institutions and the rule of law.

2. Corruption As a Response to Inadequate Governance

Weak governance structures and lack of accountability provide fertile ground for corruption to thrive. When institutions responsible for checks and balances are ineffective or compromised, individuals in positions of power can act with impunity. In such cases, corruption becomes a mechanism for personal enrichment or maintaining political control rather than a deviation from the norm.

3.   **Corruption Driven by Economic Disparities**

Economic disparities can fuel corruption as individuals seek to bridge the gap between their socio-economic status and their aspirations. In societies with limited opportunities for upward mobility, corruption becomes an avenue for those without access to resources to secure a better future for themselves and their families. This highlights how corruption is not the root cause but a symptom of unequal distribution of wealth and opportunities.

Addressing the Root Causes

To effectively combat corruption, it is essential to understand and address its root causes rather than merely treating the symptoms. Some strategies to tackle the underlying issues include:

Strengthening Institutions and the Rule of Law

Building robust institutions that uphold the rule of law and ensure accountability is crucial. This involves developing independent judiciary systems, enhancing transparency in governance, and promoting the separation of powers. Corruption can be curbed at its source by creating a system that holds individuals accountable for their actions.

Fostering a Culture of Integrity and Ethics

Promoting ethical behaviour and integrity from an early age can help shift societal norms and reduce the acceptance of corruption. Education plays a vital role in instilling values of honesty, fairness, and transparency, creating a generation that rejects corrupt practices. Creating platforms for open discussions and public awareness campaigns can also encourage a culture of integrity.

Addressing Economic Inequalities

Tackling economic disparities is crucial in combatting corruption. Governments should strive to create inclusive economic policies that provide equal opportunities for all citizens. By reducing income inequality and ensuring access to basic services, individuals are less likely to resort to corrupt practices to survive.

Enhancing International Cooperation

Corruption is a global issue that requires international cooperation to combat effectively. Sharing best practices, exchanging information, and supporting each other in investigations and legal proceedings can strengthen the fight against corruption. International organisations, such as the United Nations and World Bank, play a vital role in coordinating efforts and providing technical assistance to needy countries.

Conclusion

In conclusion, corruption is not the root cause of societal problems but rather a symptom of deeper underlying issues. Addressing corruption solely as an isolated problem will not yield long-term solutions. To effectively combat corruption, it is imperative to tackle the root causes, such as weak governance, societal norms, economic disparities, and lack of accountability. By implementing strategies that address these underlying issues, societies can create a more just and equitable future. Corruption is a symptom, not a root cause, and it is only by addressing the root causes that we can hope to eradicate this pervasive problem from our societies.

Corruption is a symptom, not a root cause. It is crucial to recognise this fact and work towards comprehensive solutions that tackle the underlying issues contributing to corruption.

Strategic Investment in Youth for Fast-Tracked National Development

Strategic investment in youths for fast-tracked national development is crucial to any nation's progress. The youth population represents a country's future, and their development and empowerment are vital for sustainable growth. By investing in the education, skills, and opportunities of young people, nations can ensure a prosperous and successful future. This chapter explores the importance of strategic investment in youths and how it can lead to fast-tracked national development.

The Power of Youth

Youth is a period of life filled with energy, enthusiasm, and potential. Harnessing this power can significantly impact a nation's development. Strategic investment in youths involves providing them with quality education, vocational training, and mentorship programs. By equipping young people with the necessary skills and knowledge, they become valuable assets in driving innovation, economic growth, and social progress.

Key Benefits of Investing in Youths

Strategic investment in youths brings a multitude of benefits to a nation. Some key advantages include:

- **Economic Growth**: When young people are empowered with education and skills, they become more employable and can contribute to the nation's economy. Increased employment opportunities increase productivity, consumer spending, and overall economic growth.

- **Innovation and Entrepreneurship**: Young minds are often filled with creative ideas and fresh perspectives. By investing in youths, nations can tap into this wellspring of innovation and entrepreneurship. Supporting young entrepreneurs and providing them with the necessary resources can lead to developing new industries, job creation, and increased competitiveness in the global market.

- **Social Development**: Investing in youths promotes social development by ensuring equal opportunities for all. By focusing on marginalised and vulnerable groups, such as girls, rural communities, and underprivileged youth, nations can bridge the social gap and promote inclusivity. This, in turn, leads to a more cohesive society and reduces social inequalities.

- **Political Stability**: Engaging young people in the development process fosters a sense of ownership and responsibility towards their nation. When youths are actively involved in decision-making processes, they become stakeholders in their country's future. This participation enhances political stability and strengthens democratic institutions.

Successful Examples of Strategic Investment in Youths

Many nations have recognised the importance of investing in youths and have implemented successful programs to fast-track national development. Some notable examples include:

1.   **South Korea**: South Korea's impressive economic growth can be attributed, in part, to its strategic investment in education and skills development. The country prioritised education, resulting in a highly skilled workforce that

contributed to the rapid growth of industries such as technology and manufacturing.

2.	**Rwanda**: Despite facing significant challenges, Rwanda has made remarkable progress in recent years. The country invested heavily in its youth population, focusing on education, skills training, and entrepreneurship. This investment has led to increased employment rates and economic growth.

3.	**Germany**: Germany's dual education system, which combines classroom learning with practical work experience, has been instrumental in shaping a highly skilled workforce. This strategic investment in youths has contributed to Germany's position as a global leader in innovation and manufacturing.

The Way Forward

Governments and stakeholders must adopt a holistic approach to ensure fast-tracked national development through strategic investment in youths. Some key steps include:

1.	**Quality Education**: Investing in quality education, from primary to tertiary levels, is essential. This includes improving infrastructure, providing trained teachers, and incorporating relevant curricula that align with industry needs.

2.	**Skills Development**: It is crucial to equip young people with practical skills that are in demand. This can be achieved through vocational training programs, apprenticeships, and internships that bridge the gap between education and employment.

3.	**Access to Opportunities**: It is vital to ensure equal access to opportunities for all youths, regardless of their socio-economic backgrounds. This involves providing scholarships, grants, and financial support to those in need.

4.   **Mentorship and Guidance**: Establishing mentorship programs that connect young people with experienced professionals can provide valuable guidance and support. Mentors can help youths navigate their career paths, build networks, and develop essential skills.

In conclusion, strategic investment in youth for fast-tracked national development is a transformative approach that can lead to sustainable growth and prosperity. By prioritising education, skills development, and equal opportunities, nations can unlock the potential of their youth population. Governments and stakeholders must recognise the power of young people and invest in their future. Only by doing so can we ensure our nations a bright and successful future.

Strategic investment in youth for fast-tracked national development is not just an option but a necessity for any nation that aspires to achieve rapid progress and sustainable development. Let us prioritise the empowerment and development of our youth, for they are the key to our nation's success.

A Final Word on Promoting National Integration

National integration is a crucial aspect of any thriving society. It involves fostering a sense of unity, harmony, and shared identity among the diverse groups that make up a nation. Promoting national integration becomes even more imperative in a world marked by increasing divisions and conflicts. This chapter will discuss some key strategies and initiatives that can contribute to promoting national integration.

Understanding the Importance

National integration is essential for a country's progress and stability. It ensures that people from different regions, ethnicities, religions, and cultures can coexist peacefully and work towards common goals. When a nation is integrated, it becomes stronger and more resilient as the collective strengths of its diverse population are harnessed. By promoting national integration, a country can safeguard against social unrest and conflicts arising from divisions and differences.

Strategies for Promoting National Integration

Governments, communities, and individuals can undertake several strategies and initiatives to promote national integration. Here are some effective approaches:

Education and Awareness

• **Education** plays a crucial role in promoting national integration. Schools and educational institutions should prioritise teaching subjects that promote understanding, tolerance, and empathy among students. Education should also include the history, traditions, and cultures of different regions and communities within the nation.

• **Awareness campaigns** can be organised to highlight the importance of national integration and its benefits. These campaigns can be conducted through various media, such as television, radio, social media, and community events. This brings us to the point where the National Orientation Agency needs a complete overhaul.

Celebrating Diversity

• **Celebrating diversity** is an effective way to foster national integration. National holidays and events can be used as platforms to showcase the rich cultural heritage of different communities. Cultural festivals, exhibitions, and performances can be organised to promote appreciation and understanding of diverse traditions.

Social Programs and Initiatives

• **Social programs** encouraging interaction and collaboration among different communities can help bridge gaps and foster unity. Volunteering activities, sports events, and community projects can bring people from diverse backgrounds together, enabling them to work towards a shared goal.

• **Initiatives that promote inclusivity and equal opportunities** are also vital for national integration. Ensuring equal access to education, healthcare, employment, and justice for all citizens helps create a fair and harmonious society.

Dialogue and Communication

• **Open dialogue and communication** are key to promoting national integration. Platforms for dialogue, such as town hall meetings, public forums, and online discussions, can be established to encourage people to express their opinions, concerns, and ideas. This enables individuals from different backgrounds to engage in meaningful conversations and find common ground.

A Final Word

In conclusion, national integration is crucial for creating a unified and prosperous nation. By implementing strategies such as education and awareness, celebrating diversity, social programs, and fostering dialogue, we can promote national integration and build a society where all citizens feel valued and included. It is essential for governments, communities, and individuals to work towards this goal collectively. Let us remember that in a world marked by divisions, promoting national integration is not just an ideal but a necessity. A final word on promoting national integration is that it is the foundation for a harmonious and inclusive society.